D1575824

Neil Armstrong

Copyright © 2015 by Quelle Histoire / quellehistoire.com
Published by Roaring Brook Press
Roaring Brook Press is a division of Holtzbrinck Publishing Holdings Limited Partnership
175 Fifth Avenue, New York, NY 10010
mackids.com

Library of Congress Control Number: 2017957517
ISBN 978-1-250-16619-7

Our books may be purchased in bulk for promotional, educational, or business use. Please contact your
local bookseller or the Macmillan Corporate and Premium Sales Department at (800) 221-7945 ext. 5442
or by e-mail at MacmillanSpecialMarkets@macmillan.com.

First published in France in 2015 by Quelle Histoire, Paris
First U.S. edition, 2018

Text: Patricia Crété
Translation: Catherine Nolan
Illustrations: Bruno Wennagel, Mathieu Ferret, Aurélie Verdon

Printed in China by RR Donnelley Asia Printing Solutions Ltd., Dongguan City, Guangdong Province
10 9 8 7 6 5 4 3 2 1

Neil Armstrong

Roaring Brook Press
New York

Future Pilot

Neil Armstrong was born in Ohio in 1930. He saw his first airplane when he was two years old. Right away, Neil knew he wanted to fly!

―――

1930–1932

Studies

Neil got his pilot's license at age sixteen—even before he got his driver's license.

After high school, he went to Purdue University. The U.S. Navy paid for his studies. In return, Neil agreed to serve as a pilot in the navy.

———

1946–1949

Navy

Neil got a call in 1949. The navy needed him.

Neil spent months training. He learned to fly jet fighters and land them on aircraft carriers.

Then Neil was sent to Korea. He flew seventy-eight missions in the Korean War, and he received three medals for his service.

———

1949–1952

Test Pilot

After the war, Neil became a test pilot. He tried out new kinds of airplanes, including super-fast rocket planes.

It was a dangerous job. Once, an engine exploded in a plane Neil was testing. Another time, the landing gear failed. Neil made it through without a scrape.

_____

1955–1960

Space Race

Neil was one of the best pilots in the country. In 1962, he was invited to become an astronaut!

The United States was in a "space race" with another country, the Soviet Union. So far, the Soviets were ahead. They had already sent the first living creature into space, a dog named Laika. They had sent the first man, too, Yuri Gagarin.

President Kennedy set a goal for the United States: the first person on the moon would be American.

1961–1962

Training

Neil and the other astronauts began training for the moon mission. There was a lot to do.

They learned to fly a spacecraft. They studied geology so they could make reports about the moon's surface. They worked underwater in their space suits, to prepare for floating around in space.

They even learned how to kill and eat a snake. Why? In case they landed in the wilderness when they flew back to Earth!

——

1963–1968

Blast Off

On July 16, 1969, three astronauts climbed into a tall rocket. Neil was the commander. He was joined by Edwin "Buzz" Aldrin and Michael Collins.

The astronauts blasted off, leaving a fiery trail behind them. Next stop, the moon!

_____

July 16, 1969

Walking on the Moon

Four days later, the astronauts reached their destination.

Around the world, half a billion people watched on TV. They held their breath as Neil opened the door of the spacecraft. They watched him take a step—the very first step on the moon.

"That's one small step for man," said Neil, "one giant leap for mankind."

———

July 20, 1969

The Return

The astronauts took photos, collected rocks, and planted the American flag—all while the world watched.

After twenty-one hours, it was time to go home. The three men returned to Earth aboard the *Apollo 11*. They landed on July 24, 1969.

Neil, Buzz, and Michael were heroes. Everywhere they went, people clapped and cheered.

———

July 24, 1969

The Last Years

Neil retired from his position as an astronaut two years later. But he wasn't done working. He went on to become a professor, a businessman, and a dairy farmer. He bought his own farm in his home state, Ohio.

Neil died on August 25, 2012. He will be remembered always as the first man to walk on the moon.

———

1971–2012

1930
Born in
Wapakoneta,
Ohio.

1956
Marries Janet
Shearon.

1958
NASA, the group
that runs the
space program,
is formed.

1965
Neil commands
a mission called
Gemini 8, which
orbits Earth.

1920

1951
Starts serving
in the navy.

1957
First flight in a
rocket plane.

1961
NASA starts
planning the
mission to the
moon.

1969
Neil is chosen
for the Apollo 11
moon mission.

1969
Walks on the moon.

1979
Makes an ad for Chrysler cars.

1994
Marries his second wife, Carol Held Knight.

2012
Neil's ashes are scattered in the Atlantic Ocean.

2015

1971
Leaves space program to teach.

1986
Helps investigate a space shuttle explosion.

2012
Dies following heart surgery.

The United States

CANADA

UNITED STATES

MEXICO

MAP KEY

1 Wapakoneta, Ohio

This is Neil's birthplace and the site of a space museum created in his honor.

2 Pensacola, Florida

The city is home to the largest U.S. Naval Air Station.

3 Edwards Air Force Base

The U.S. Air Force uses this base, located in a California desert, for aircraft and rocket tests.

4 Cape Canaveral

Many spacecraft have launched from the air force station here and from Kennedy Space Center on nearby Merritt Island, Florida.

5 Cincinnati, Ohio

Neil taught at a university here from 1971 to 1979.

6 Lebanon, Ohio

Neil bought and ran a dairy farm in this small village.

People to Know

John Fitzgerald Kennedy
(1917–1963)
John was the thirty-fifth president of the United States. He dreamed of having an American be the first to walk on the moon, but he was killed before he could see his dream come true.

Janet Elizabeth Shearon
(Born in 1934)
Neil met Janet, his first wife, in college. They had three children: Eric, Karen, and Mark. They divorced in 1994.

General Matthew Ridgway

(1895–1993)

This American soldier served in World War I, World War II, and the Korean War. Neil served under his command in Korea.

Charles Lindbergh

(1902–1974)

Charles was the first pilot to fly solo nonstop from New York to Paris. Neil admired him, and the two men met several times.

....

Many of Neil's space artifacts are housed at the Smithsonian, in Washington, DC.

....

The footprints that Neil and Buzz left on the moon are still there. There's no wind to blow them away.

....

When Neil was ten, he had a job mowing the lawn at the local cemetery. He earned one dollar per hour.

....

Neil was an Eagle Scout. He also played baritone horn in a band.

Available Now

 Muhammad Ali

 Neil Armstrong

 Blackbeard

 Coco Chanel

 Charlie Chaplin

 Cleopatra

 Marie Curie

 Albert Einstein

 Abraham Lincoln

 Nelson Mandela

 Isaac Newton

 Rosa Parks

Coming Soon

 Anne Frank

 Gandhi

 Frida Kahlo

 Martin Luther King, Jr.